12 Tips To Achieve Financial Freedom

The Simple Guide To Successfully Manage Your
Personal Finance

By James Justin

Dedication

This manuscript is dedicated to my wife, Dr. Lauretta Justin. Without you, I would not be who I am, and this book would not be a reality. Thank you for challenging me to think bigger. I love you always!

To my three sons: Nathan, Sean and Joshua. Thank you for teaching me the true meaning of patience. Remember, together we will make a difference in the world!

To my parents: Thank you for all your love and support. My success, joy and happiness are possible because of your sacrifices and your decision to move from Haiti to the United States. Thank you!

Acknowledgement

Special thank you to my editors, Mark Wahlton and Dr. Lauretta Justin! This book is a reality because of your brilliance. Thank you for partnership!

Table of Contents

Tip #1

Change your Mindset, Change your Life

Recently, I was talking with my friend John, and he asked me the following question: "Do you ever feel like you're not going to make it financially?"

I told John that I used to worry about that all the time, but not anymore. I have things under control now since I discovered the following financial freedom secrets:

- I learned that Financial Freedom is a choice, and that **choice** begins in my mind.

- I learned that it is not about how much money I *earn*; it's about how much money I ***keep***!

- I also learned that financial freedom is not so much about money itself, but it's about owning my time and my life. It's about the freedom I gain to enjoy everyday life with my loved ones without the worries of basic financial needs!

I explained to John that my financial status improved primarily because I had changed the way I think about money. And since I think differently about money, I manage my finances differently. Subsequently, I get favorable results.

"I wish I could say that," John said. "I just feel like I'm never going to make enough money."

John is a regional manager for a large company. He brings home a six figure salary, lives in a nice neighborhood and drives a nice Lexus. He's a hard worker and a great provider for his family. John is one of the good guys and he's a great friend. From the outside John looks like he's living the American dream. So why was he struggling?

Simple: John FELT he was NEVER going to make enough money. The reality is that money was not John's biggest problem. It was his *thinking*. The limited belief he had about money kept him poor, even though he earned a lot more money than most of my coaching clients who are financially free.

After a few months of coaching with John, he was able to dramatically change his financial situation. John was committed to creating a happier life for himself and his family. Together we worked on the following goals:

- Redefining his life mission

- Reframing his limited belief about money

- Setting smart financial goals

- Developing a strategic plan to achieve his objectives

- Automating his personal finance

In our coaching process, John realized the obstacles impeding his financial progress. Ultimately, I helped John change his **MONEY MINDSET** to transform his life and his personal finance. In the notes section of this book, I provided 5 tips below on how you can change your money mindset. Also, I highly recommend that you review all the notes at the end of this book and read my new book, "**Mindset: How to transform your life from ordinary to extraordinary**."

Now, John is able to keep more of the money he earns to cover his expenses. He is also able to give money to his favorite charities, save and invest.   And most importantly, John is able to spend more time with his family. Although John is still bringing home the same income, he now knows how to effectively manage his money for maximum impact. John is well on his way to financial freedom!

Wow...what an inspiring story!

And I believe if John can do it, so can **YOU**!

I believe in YOU! And I encourage you to pursue your goals!

As you begin your path to financial freedom, I encourage you to meditate on the following success formula:

Positive Mindset + Positive Actions = Positive Results

I believe that if you change your mindset, you **WILL** change your life! I am a living witness and testament to that success concept. As you continue to adopt a positive mindset and follow the tips outlined in this book, you will achieve your goals.

How to Change your Money Mindset

1. Acknowledge your current thinking about money by taking a brief inventory of your money history. Ask your financial planners for help as needed. This process will help you identify how you have developed your belief about money, wealth and financial freedom. *Your Belief system determines your Mindset; your Mindset determines your Feelings; your Feelings determine your Actions and your Actions determine your Results.*

2. Recognize that you have a choice, and that you, too, will become wealthy as you practice the tips in this program. You have the power to be financially free!

3. Commit to financial literacy to replace your limited belief about money and wealth. The more you learn... the more you earn.

4. Develop a smart plan with your financial advisors and take action toward your financial goals. Automate your financial freedom plan. This process will help you remain faithful to your plan. For example, if your income is $1000 per week; give $100 to your favorite charities; invest $100 to grow your money; save $100 for fun and for emergencies; and live on the remaining $700.

5. Appreciate what you have *now* while you pursue a bigger financial portfolio. An attitude of gratitude will ensure that you are happy and fulfilled at all times.

"Be thankful for what you have; you'll end up having more. If you concentrate on what you don't have, you will never, ever have enough.
Oprah Winphrey

As with John, if you change your limited THINKING, and practice the Financial Freedom tips in this program, you'll be well on your way to become financially free and transform your life! For individual or corporate coaching, visit CoachJamesJustin.com and send me an email today!

Tip #2

Define what Financial Freedom means to you based on your core values

"Financial Freedom isn't about how much money you make, it's about how much you keep, and the freedom you gain to enjoy everyday life."
James Justin

Financial Freedom means different things to different people. For some people, it's about freedom of time. For others, it's about having lots of money in the bank. That is why I am encouraging you to define what Financial Freedom means to **YOU**. This is an important step toward achieving your financial goals. When you have your own definition, you'll have focus and clarity.

There is a misconception that having an abundance of money gives you freedom. However, I can give you real life examples from my coaching clients who have an abundance of income and wealth, but continue to feel like they are sinking in quicksand.

In contrast, I can share examples of people with a modest income and home who consider themselves financially free. Better yet, there are people generating meager incomes, but since they are doing what they love, they feel great! They are happy and are financially free!

As an entrepreneur, speaker and life coach who works with all kinds of people, I can easily say that Financial

Freedom represents more than money. It's a mindset. It's an attitude.

The day I changed my limited thinking about money, defined what financial freedom means to me and took action toward my goals, I began to *attract* money instead of *repelling* it. Likewise, if you define what Financial Freedom means to you and pursue it, you will have similar results.

What Is Financial Freedom?

Financial Freedom is what you want from life, and it doesn't necessarily have to revolve solely around money.

> *"Financial Freedom is much more than having money. It's the freedom to be who you really are and do what you really want in life."*
>
> *richdad.com*

Here's another way to define Financial Freedom: Invest your money wisely, save and spend your money according to your core values. When you've successfully invested in your nest egg, it can grow exponentially so much so that the interest earned from your investments may even replace your current income.

For example, several years ago my wife and I started a business (Millennium Eye Center). Over the years the business has grown and now generates enough money to support us and allow us to have the freedom of time. This business has become our little golden goose! As long as we keep this Golden Goose systematically alive, we'll enjoy this continuous flow of income, allowing us to focus on our core values without constantly worrying about basic expenses. This continuous flow of income has allowed us to enjoy everyday life with our family. For my wife and I, Financial Freedom is about owning our time.

Based on those very broad definitions of Financial Freedom, is it clear that the term means different things to different people. Someone may want to travel around the world. And in order to do that, they sell all of their possessions. To them, they are financially free to do what they want.

Another person may want to work from home so that they may be able to see their children more frequently. As you can see, there are so many different values, motives, and means to obtain and enjoy Financial Freedom. What is your definition of Financial Freedom?

How you define *yours* is personal and totally up to you. I recommend that you develop your definition around your core values.

Core Values

My challenge to you is to define your path to Financial Freedom. Define your Financial Freedom based on your core values. Understand that you will not be financially free overnight. However, if you are able to define what Financial Freedom means to you based on what's important to you, you'll be well on your way toward financial independence. If you are just coasting along, not knowing what you are striving for, you are going to lose focus and fall back into the same unproductive cycle.

"At the end of the day, the position is just a position, a title is just a title, and those things come and go. It's really your essence and your values that are important."
Queen Rania of Jordan

Your core values are essential for lasting success. They are the foundation that guides your decisions in life. They are the things that are dear to your heart.

Your values begin in your mind. They are shaped by the stories you tell yourself. They are based on the stories that you believe in and that you accept as being true and accurate.

My core values include faith, family, friends, finances, fitness (spirit, soul, and body), and fun. I allocate my funds based on my values, and I recommend the same for you.

In your pursuit of Financial Freedom, it's important to first determine your values; and let them guide your decisions. For example, if integrity is important to you, then act accordingly, and be sure to surround yourself with people of integrity, since a chain is only as strong as its weakest link. Let your values guide your financial decisions and seek Financial Freedom with integrity!

I encourage you to define what financial freedom means to you based upon your core values and take 1 action every day to achieve it. This process will give you clarity and direction. To get started, here is a quote to consider:

"My definition of FINANCIAL FREEDOM is simple: It is the ability to live the lifestyle you desire without having to work or rely on anyone else for money."

T. Harv Eker

Tip #3

Become Financially Literate

> *"I believe that through knowledge
> and discipline, financial peace is
> possible for all of us."*
>
> Dave Ramsey

Financial literacy is the process of understanding how money works, how someone manages to earn or make it, how that person manages it, how they invest it (turn it into more) and how that person donates it to help others.

Financial literacy may include topics such as personal finance, earning, giving, saving, investing, real estate, insurance, tax planning and retirement.

It also involves a general knowledge of financial concepts including financial planning, expenses, income, assets, liability, compound interest, debt, credit card management and consumer rights.

The National Financial Educators Council defines financial literacy as: *"Possessing the skills and knowledge on financial matters to confidently take effective action that best fulfills an individual's personal, family and global community goals."*

Financial literacy is important because it's the foundation for Financial Freedom. Without such, knowledge, skills, abilities and discipline, you will not be able to manage your wealth effectively. And if *you* don't manage your money, it will soon manage you. One of the best ways to manage your money is to track it.

You may have heard of people who won millions overnight in the lottery, only to lose it all in less than a year. Do you know why? One of the reasons is due to lack of financial literacy, experience, and discipline. They simply lacked the financial literacy to manage their new-found money effectively. If you want to achieve Financial Freedom, you must commit to financial literacy and take actions toward your goals.

7 Pillars of Financial Literacy

"We were not taught financial literacy in school. It takes a lot of work and time to change your thinking and to become financially literate."

Robert Kiyosaki

According to Robert Kiyosaki, there are five pillars to financial literacy. And I'm going to give you two more as a bonus! These pillars are the cornerstone of your Financial Freedom. If you learn the basics of these pillars, you will transform your finances and your life.

1. Economics
2. Accounting
3. Taxes
4. Investing
5. Building businesses
6. Commitment to continued growth and development
7. Giving back

Financial literacy is an ongoing learning process. To help you get started I recommend several books on the subject in the reference list. Be sure to review the provided resources, read the books and apply what you learn to transform your finances and your life.

Tip #4

Identify Your Current Financial Status

"Before you can improve your financial status, you must first identify where you are now, develop a plan to achieve your goal and follow the plan."

James Justin

Do you know what your current financial status is? By that I mean can you readily answer the following financial statement questions:

- What is my net worth?
- What is my FICO score?
- What is the total value of my assets?
- What are my liabilities and their current payoff amount?
- How much do I earn?
- How much do I spend?
- Do I have adequate insurance coverage and legal protection?

Can you get the answers to these questions? If you have the answers to the questions above, congratulations! You are well on your way to Financial Freedom! I recommend keeping or compiling these documents in a central place. Store your financial documents (both electronic or paper) in a safe place where you can quickly find them.

If you can't readily answer the financial statement questions above, now is the time to stop and take stock of your finances. The primary goal is to dig deeper to reveal your actual assets, liabilities, income and expenses. If you don't know your current financial status, how can you ever determine where you want to go tomorrow?

Before you can achieve Financial Freedom you must first determine why you are where you are financially. Then, you must develop a definite plan to get where you want to be. Most plans fail because of lack of council. Therefore, get help from certified financial advisors to help you develop your financial plan.

Here's the good news: You can transform your personal finance! You can (and must) start right where you are. Let's walk you through each of the preceding financial statement questions:

What is my net worth?

Net worth (sometimes called net wealth) is the total assets minus total liabilities of an individual or a company. This is actually a question you will be able to answer after you answer all the subsequent questions. What your financial net worth represents is the total value of your assets, minus the total value of your liabilities. If you have a positive net worth, that is great! The higher it is, the better off you are in terms of financial independence.

If you have a negative net worth, don't sweat it. Don't even worry about it. *You have the power to reverse it!* Many people have, and it is not an insurmountable obstacle. If they can do it, so can you!

18

As you answer the subsequent questions, you'll have a better idea of your financial net worth. This new found knowledge and understanding of your current financial statement will put you in the path to financial freedom.

What is my FICO score?

This score is based on the model developed by the Fair Issac Corporation (FICO). It's a way of measuring an individual's creditworthiness. A FICO score is a quantification of a variety of factors in an individual's background including a history of default, the current amount of debt and the length of time that the individual has made purchases on credit.

A FICO score ranges between 350 and 850. In general, a score of 650 is considered a "fair" credit score, while 750 or higher is considered "excellent." A FICO score is a convenient way to summarize an individual's credit history. Your FICO score is...

- A history of how you obtain and manage debts
- A history of your demographic (places where you lived).

You can get a free annual credit report online. However, if you want to get your FICO score, you'll have to pay a fee to the credit bureaus. In the U.S.A, there are 3 major credit bureaus:

1. Equifax: Phone # 1-866-349-5191
2. Experian: Phone # 1-888-397-3742
3. TransUnion: Phone # 1-800-916-8800

These agencies collect information about you, compile a file and keep it on their database computer.

Free Credit Reports

It is imperative that you obtain your credit reports from each of the three credit reporting agencies at least annually so that you can monitor your credit report. Financial Freedom mandates that *you* know what these agencies know (or think they know) about your credit history, especially since these agencies are sharing this information with potential creditors.

Unfortunately, these reports often contain erroneous information resulting in higher costs for things such as loans and insurance for millions of Americans. The credit reporting agencies must legally provide you a copy of your credit report free of charge once per year. You can request all three reports at once, or space them out throughout the year. To request your free credit report online, visit AnnualCreditReport.com or call 1-877-322-8228.

What is the value of my assets?

An asset is anything you own that has value. Things that fall into this category include:

- Bank accounts such as savings, CDs, money markets, etc.
- Investment accounts such as mutual funds, stocks, bonds and monies obtained from business investments

20

- Tangible personal property such as houses, cars, boats, art, collectibles, etc.
- Intellectual property such as loyalty money obtained from ideas or products you sell or license to others such as books, online courses, etc.

In this era of electronic commerce, almost anything can have value. If you own anything that people want, it has a value. A cursory online search can help you determine the going price for similar items. I recommend that you focus on the current value of big-ticket items in calculating your net worth. For example, while the new car you bought in 2015 may have cost you $25,000, its current value may only be $15,000.

Assets may also include your investment in a business that you own, especially if it is the type of business that can be sold. Factor this into your calculation as well, but remember in all things to be conservative. In other words, it is better to underestimate something's value than to overestimate it.

What are all my liabilities and their current payoff amounts?

This is much like the assets exercise except this time you are determining your liabilities, the things on which you owe money. This traditionally includes balances on all forms of debt such as credit cards, loans, mortgages and home equity lines of credit. Your financial liability is the total amount it would currently cost to pay all of your debts.

How much do I earn?

Do you know what your current fully loaded salary is? Fully loaded value is determined by adding your base salary plus any benefits offered by your employer or your company. If you own your own business, do you know what your current revenues are, both gross and net (after expenses)?

Get clear on exactly how much you are earning both before and after taxes to obtain a snapshot of your cash inflow.

How much do I spend?

Take a look at the last twelve months of expenses to determine where your money is going. If you can't readily track your previous twelve month expenses, make a good estimate by referencing your checkbook register, credit cards and bank statements. Then, going forward, start tracking every dime you spend.

There are some good online tools for doing this, as well as programs you can download. For example, I use Intuit Quicken software for personal finance, and QuickBooks for our businesses. You can use any free online software as well. If you need help deciding which money tracking tool is best for you, email me by visiting CoachJamesJustin.com.

I want you to start tracking where your money is going! Again, Financial Freedom is not about how much money you *make*; it's how much you *keep*.

Taking control of where your money is going is a major step to keep your money. If you don't track your money, you cannot manage it. If you don't manage your money, you'll eventually lose it.

Are my assets insured and legally protected?

It is important that you realize the value of insurance in protecting your personal and business finances. This includes life insurance, car insurance, business liability insurance, health insurance, home insurance, disability insurance, and renter's insurance. The goal is to be adequately protected without making yourself insurance poor.

Legally speaking, you want to make sure you have the proper documents in place to protect you while you are alive, as well as when you die. This includes wills, powers of attorney and asset distribution upon your death. The services of a good attorney will assist you with this.

Tip #5

Set Your Financial Goals and Take Action to Achieve Them

"Successful people maintain a positive focus in life no matter what is going on around them. They stay focused on their past successes rather than their past failures, and on the next action steps they need to take to get them closer to the fulfillment of their goals rather than all the other distractions that life presents to them."

Jack Canfield

What are your financial goals? Once you've determined your current financial status, the next step is to set smart goals with objectives to get where you want to be. Take some time to imagine being financially free and write down whatsoever comes to mind. How would you feel to know that you have achieved your financial goals? What would you do with your new found wealth?

Now, write down 1 to 4 goals you would like to achieve in your pursuit of Financial Freedom. This can include your investment, giving, saving and spending goals. For each goal you write down, include the action steps required to achieve it. For example, I want to save $4,980 by January 31, 2017 for my retirement. To achieve this goal, I'll do the following:

- Open an individual retirement account (IRA) by January 31

- Fund my IRA account by $415 per month via direct deposit. This will help me avoid procrastination and forgetfulness.
- Review my quarterly statement and track my money.

Break your goals down into 1-, 3-, 5- and 10-year goals. Then, next to each goal answer the question: "Am I willing to do what it takes to achieve the goals? When I achieve this goal what will that mean to me and how will I feel? What will I have *then* that I do not have *now*?"

Make note of all your answers, as they will provide important information to use as inspiration and milestones along the way. We are here to help you! One of our financial planners, accountants and lawyers is happy to help you achieve your financial goals. All you have to do is ask. We are only a call or click away. Contact us today by visiting CoachJamesJustin.com!

Tip #6

Take Some Risk to Achieve Your Financial Goals

"Never test the depth of a river with both feet."
Warren Buffet

Taking risk is part of life. We cannot avoid it. If we stop taking risk, we stop living. The good news is that taking risk does not have to be a negative experience. We can learn to take smarter risks for greater rewards. Let's explore some of the ways to do that.

The process of becoming financially free *does* requires some risk. However, the reward is far greater than the risk. For example, it was risky for me to use my savings to start my business, but if I did not make that decision, I wouldn't be financially free today. In my opinion, the best ways to become financially free is to invest, invest and invest. The same is true for you. If you want to achieve your Financial Freedom you must take some risk by investing some of your money.

The key to any risk management is doing your homework, seeking coaching from professionals and taking risks that you can afford. You can always adjust your risk level as you become more knowledgeable about financial literacy and able to aim higher toward your financial goals.

I encourage you to celebrate every progress you made big and small. Have a big party or do something small to celebrate your wins. And take time off to show gratitude to those who helped you achieve your goals.

Tip #7

Learn to Manage Your Debt

"Whether your debt is good or bad depends on the type of debt, the reason you owe it, and whether you can afford to repay it. When used the right way, debt can help you manage your finances more effectively, leverage your wealth, buy things you need, and handle emergencies."
John Ventura and Mary Reed from the book Managing Debt for Dummies

While debt can cause you to be stressed, it can also help you build wealth. Why is that? Well, all debts are not equal. There's a difference between good debt and bad debt. Good debt helps increase your financial net worth, whereas bad debt decreases it.

Good debt can help you:

- Build your family's financial net worth.
- Invest in a business to make money for years to come.
- Invest in yourself in order to increase your earnings potential, and to develop yourself personally and professionally. Student loans are a common example of this kind of debt.

On the other hand, bad debt causes you to:

- Go into debt to buy nonessential goods or services that do not increase your wealth, and have no lasting value. Examples include restaurant meals, groceries, clothing, personal items and vacations.

- Have a high interest rate debt and make low monthly payments. By the time you pay off the debt, the amount you pay in interest exceeds the value of the product or service you financed.

- Borrow money from dangerous lenders such as advance fee lenders or payday lenders, and writing checks against your credit card that you struggle to pay off in full.

Your Financial Freedom begins in your MIND. Don't let bad debt control your life. One of the best ways to use debt effectively is to invest it into a business or something that will give you an ongoing return on investment (ROI).

5 Tips to pay off your debts faster

One of the best ways to use debt effectively is to invest it into a business or something that will give you an inflow of income for years.

Managing and paying off negative debts are important steps to Financial Freedom. However, if you want to pay off your debts faster, you'll need a plan. Here are five tips to get started:

1.   Pay yourself first. Send money to your saving or investment account before paying anyone.

2.   Gather all your debts and record them in your book-keeping or accounting software such as Quicken or Mint.com.

3.   Call your creditors and ask for a lower interest rate. You never know unless you ask; and if you ask, you may get a lower rate. You can also ask for better payment options.

4.   Target one debt at a time, pay more than the minimum amount due and activate direct-deposit payments to avoid late fees.

5.   Get help from a professional and become financially literate!

Money is an idea. It's a tool used to exchange goods or services. The money you borrow is called a debt. A debt can be good or bad. It's can help you build wealth or cause financial problems. Good debts increase your assets while bad debts increase your liabilities. To pay off your debts faster, follow the 5 tips provided in this module.

Tip #8

Create Multiple Streams of Income

> *"Never depend on a single income. Make investments to create a second source."*
>
> Warren Buffet

Creating multiple streams of income is an important step toward your Financial Freedom. The same way you need two legs to stand securely, you need a minimum of two sources of income to obtain basic financial security.

Why do you need multiple sources of incomes? Well, because we can't control life! You can lose your job or business at any time. If you have another income source, at least you'll be able to meet your needs until you bounce back.

5 Tips to Make More Money

1. Sell your unwanted stuff online at amazon.com, craigslist.com, or similar websites. You can also have a garage sale. All the extra cash you generate must be placed in your investment account to create other opportunities to make more money.

2. Ask your boss for a raise, especially if you have been a valuable employee and continually helped the company increase their revenue. It may be time to re-negotiate for a higher salary. You never know, your boss may grant your request. If you

need coaching on how to ask for a raise, email me for more tips by visiting CoachJamesJustin.com.

3. Start a blog and a website to share your advice, experiences and expertise. With enough material and a substantial list of loyal followers, you can sell them your products and services. The more people you help get what *they* want; the more people will help you get what *you* want! Ziz Ziglar

4. Invest, Invest and Invest. This is the best way to multiply your money. Invest on yourself, your business and real estate. Start with one house and rent out a room. The extra cash can be used to buy another property. Before pursuing any investment, consult your financial advisors.

5. Start a business while keeping your day job. This process will help you develop multiple streams of income. You can get started by turning your hobbies into profitable businesses. For example, if you are a teacher, you can give tutoring lessons for a fee, and automatically put that extra cash into your investment account. If you like to read, speak and write, turn your research into an eBook or other products to be sold online and offline.

Business is a major part of financial freedom. In fact, every financial transaction is a form of business. If you want to be free financially, I highly recommend that you build businesses. If you don't want to start your own business, partner with others who are successful in business.

While there are many sources of income, all income is separated into 3 types. They are as follows:

1. Earned Income

2. Portfolio Income

3. Passive Income

Earned Income means money received, in cash or in-kind, from wages, salary or commissions in exchange for the performance of services by the employee. This form of income is highly taxed by the U.S Internal Revenue Service agency. The earned income you have, the more you'll pay on taxes.

Portfolio income is income generated from investments, dividends, interest, royalties and capital gains.

Passive Income is derived from rental property, limited partnership or other enterprise in which a person is not materially involved. As with earned income, passive income is usually taxable; however, it is often treated differently by the Internal Revenue Service (IRS). Ask your accountant for details.

Creating multiple streams of income is a major part of increasing your financial portfolio. The best way to achieve that goal is to invest your money in several businesses. When you invest your money, you are more likely to get a higher return on investment (ROI) rather than just save. Consult your business and financial advisors before implementing your financial plan.

To create multiple streams of income, follow the 5 tips provided in this module. Direct your focus to generate Portfolio and Passive Incomes. These 2 types of income often give greater returns. Creating multiple streams of income by adding value to the world. The more you help people get what they want, the more they'll help you get what you want.

Tip #9

Giving Back

"It's not how much we give, but how much love we put into giving."
Mother Teresa

Giving is one of the keys to financial success and happiness. Why is that? Well, giving is the beginning of receiving. It is the law of cause and effect in action. It opens the door to prosperity.

Here are 3 steps to giving wisely:

1. Give according to your personal values and/or convictions. Giving should be from the heart. Give out of love and wisdom.

2. Give what you can afford. Start with a tithe (10% of what you have). It could be money, time or expertise.

3. Automate your giving to make it consistent using your banking Bill Pay system.

Develop a lifestyle of giving, and you'll create a path to financial success and happiness! Develop an attitude of giving. Live to give and give out of love and wisdom.

"Remember that the happiest people are not those getting more, but those giving more."
H. Jackson Brown, Jr.

Many people struggle with giving. This is especially true to give money away. Here are 3 tips I used to overcome this obstacle:

1. Select 1-3 of your favorite charities. This may include your church or local non-profit organizations.

2. Give 1-10 percent of your salary to your selected charities. If you don't have any income, you can give an hour of your time per year in volunteerism. You can also give household items such as clothing and kitchen wares. Start small and increase your giving as you get comfortable.

3. Get your loved ones to help you stay committed. An accountability partner is always helpful to have in the area that's not your strength.

Several years ago, I needed the help to give constantly. My wife was that accountability partner who ensured that I gave money to my favorite charities faithfully. She showed me the benefits of giving such as tax deductions. Now, I give automatically by using my bank Bill Pay service; and I recommend this strategy for you!

Tip #10

How to Invest Intelligently

"Do not put all your eggs in one basket."
Warren Buffet

One of the reasons why people invest their money is to make a profit and to multiply their money. This is how you can make your money work hard for you instead of you working hard for it.

What's investment? According to investopedia.com, financial investment is the purchase of goods that are used to create wealth over time. When it comes to investing your money, it's important to do it strategically by following the patterns of successful investors such as Warren Buffet. Before you start any financial plan, I recommend that you consult your financial advisors.

Why many people don't invest? Fear of losing money is the primary reason why many people don't invest their money. They are afraid of losing their entire funds.

Here are 5 tips to consider before you invest your money:

1. Decide why you want to invest
2. Determine your risk tolerance
3. Commit to financial literacy
4. Hire a financial advisor
5. Know the fees on your investment transactions

Where do the rich invest their money?

"The philosophy of the rich and the poor is this: the rich invest their money and spend what is left. The poor spend their money and invest what is left."
Robert Kiyosaki

The latest World Wealth Report from Capgemini and RBC Wealth Management came out recently, and it had some important insights on where and how the world's ultra-rich are investing their millions. Last year, high-net-worth individuals, or HNWIs (defined as people with investable assets of $1 million or more, excluding primary residence, collectibles, consumables, and consumer durables), became slightly riskier: Stocks overtook cash as the No. 1 asset in their portfolios. Other investment assets include fixed income, real estate, cash on cash equivalents and equities. (Businessinsider.com).

The ultimate key to Financial Freedom is to first invest in yourself, and then invest your money. Here's my recommendation:

1. First invest in yourself. Why? Because **YOU** are your best asset! You can start by getting a professional life coach to help you develop yourself personally and professionally.

2. Invest in your own financial education even if you have financial advisors. You don't need a degree in finance, investment or economics to start your investment journey. You can get started by reading the books recommended in the reference section of this

program and apply what you have learned. The more you understand finance, the more you can make better informed choices.

3. Just do it! Take action today! You can invest in many assets such as your own business, stocks and real estate. However, you must take action in order to achieve your investment goals.

Knowledge is power only when it's applied to a definite goal. After you have acquired the necessary knowledge and have consulted your advisors, take immediate action to achieve your financial goals.

As you continue to implement the tips from this chapter, you'll be able to make wiser investments. You'll be able to minimize your risk. More importantly, your return on investment is often higher when you invest intelligently.

Tip #11

How to Save Wisely

"Do not save what is left after spending, but spend what is left after saving."
Warren Buffet

In the Financial Freedom journey, it does not matter how much money you make; it is how much money you **KEEP**. Saving for raining day and to invest will help you keep your money. In this section, let's focus on how to save your wealth wisely.

4 tips to save your money wisely:

1. Plan ahead. Spend 2 minutes for every $1 spend.

2. Make your saving simple and fun. Use the system in tip 3.

3. Automate your savings plan by directing all your incomes automatically to your checking account. From there, send 10% of your money to your charity account, 10% to your saving account and 10% to your investment account.

   Some of my clients find it helpful to use different banks for each of these accounts. I recommend that you manage your expenses to live within the remaining 70% income. For example, if you make $100 per week, give $10 to your favorite charities,

$10 for your saving, $10 for your investment, leaving you $70 to spend. Ask your banker and your financial advisor for help.

4. Celebrate each time you reach your goal.

Here are 10 great ways to celebrate your successes:

1. Take a deep breath.

2. Share the news with friends, family and colleagues.

3. Give your goals a one-day break.

4. Reflect on the path you took.

5. Write down your success and put it where you can see it every day.

6. Sleep in.

7. Thank everyone who supported you.

8. Tweet it.

9. Support someone else in reaching his or her goal.

10. Cross it off your master list of goals.

Saving is important. It helps you prepare for raining day or for your next vacation. Once of the best ways to increase your savings is to invest your money!

Tip #12

How to Spend Sensibly

"If you buy things you do not need, soon you'll have to sell things you need."

Warren Buffet

There are many different rules on how to control spending. I personally follow the 70/30 rule. I live on 70% of my income, give 10% to my favorite charitable organizations, invest 10% and save the remaining 10%. Don't get caught up on deciding which rule is best. Just pick one, automate it and review it quarterly.

The average income in the U.S., by household, was $63,784 in 2013, according to the Consumer Expenditure Survey conducted by the U.S. Bureau of Labor Statistics. Here's how the average household budget breaks down:

Expenses	Annual Average Cost	% of Budget
1. Housing	$10,080	16%
2. Transport.	$9,004	14%
3. Taxes	$7,432	12%
4. Utilities	$7,068	11%
5. Food	$6,602	10%

6. Social Security Contributions, Personal Insurance and Pensions

	$5,528	9%

7. Debt Payments or Savings

	$5,252	8%

8. Healthcare	$3,631	6%
9. Entertainment	$2,564	4%

10. Cash Contributions

	$1,834	3%

11. Apparel and Services

	$1,604	3%

12. Education	$1,138	2%
13. Vices	$775	1%
14. Miscellaneous	$664	1%
Personal Care	$608	1%
TOTA:	$63,784	100%

How are your expenditures compare to the average Americans? The key to spending sensibly is to spend than your income. The money you keep can be used for saving and investing.

Spending is an important part of enjoying everyday life. When you do it right, you can enjoy life without worrying about financial stress. Spending wisely add value to your life. It helps you keep your money. Here are 3 tips to spend your money sensibly:

1. Identify your core values. For example, my core values are Faith and Spirituality; Family and Friends, Fitness and Health; Finance and Fun. I strive to spend my money, time and energy around these values.

2. Develop a simple plan to spend your money on things that matter most to you. Spend 2 Minutes planning for every $1 you spend.

3. Follow the 70/30 rule discussed in the previous module of this book.

To spend your money sensibly, I recommend that you follow the 70/30 rule and let me know how it's working for you. Keep me updated via email at james@coachJamesJustin.com.

Conclusion

Financial Freedom begins in the mind. It's the process of enjoying everyday life without the need to worry about money.

More importantly, Financial Freedom is a *choice*. That choice is available to YOU! And that's great news!

It doesn't matter who you are, where you are from or what financial mistakes you have made. You can still choose to become financially free! You can choose to master your money. You can choose to make your money work hard for you instead of you working hard for it. Financial freedom is available to you! If you pursue it diligently, you'll find it!

As your success coach, I'm dedicated to helping you achieve extraordinary RESULTS! I wrote this book to help you succeed in your finances and in life. The book offers you the foundational knowledge you need to get started. As you continue to practice the 12 tips outlined in this manuscript, you'll be well on your way to becoming Financially Free!

Now that you have the foundations to start your journey to Financial Freedom, it's time to take action and achieve your financial goals!

Until next time, continue to transform your life to personal freedom from ordinary to EXTRAORDINARY! Let's get started today! Visit CoachJamesJustin.com and email me your comments or questions. I am here to help YOU!

Notes

Personal Finance

Personal finance is defined as the management of money and financial decisions for a person or family including budgeting, investments and retirement planning.

Budget

Budget is a plan used to decide the amount of money that can be spent and how it will be spent.

Income

Income is money that an individual or business receives in exchange for providing a good or service or through investing capital. Income often comes from a job or a business diligence.

Expense

It's the cost required for something; the money spent to pay a bill such as rent or home mortgage.

Asset

It's a valuable property owned by a person or company, regarded as having value and available to meet debts, commitments, or legacies. An asset is a resource with economic value that an individual, corporation or country owns or controls with the expectation that it will provide future benefit. Asset is any transaction that put money in your pocket.

Liability

A liability is a person or company's legal debt. Liability takes money out of pocket.

Retirement Planning

It's the process of determining retirement income goals and the actions and decisions necessary to achieve those goals. Retirement planning includes identifying sources of income, estimating expenses, implementing a savings program and managing assets for yourself and future generations.

Definition of Wealth

The definition of wealth is the number of days you can survive without you or anyone in your household) physically working and still maintain your standard of living. For example, if your monthly expenses are $5,000, and you have $20,000 in savings, your wealth is approximately four months, or 120 days. Wealth is measured by time and not just dollars. (richdad.com)

What Does It Mean to be Rich?

We all have our own definition of what it means to be rich. This is because we are unique with particular needs and wants. Here's a simple definition of rich: "having a lot of money and possessions; having or supplying a large amount of something that is wanted or needed" (Merriam-Webster Dictionary).

Millionaire Mindset

The major difference between people who are financially free and those who are not is their MINDSET. The way we think is important because it affects our feelings, our actions and our results. If we want to change our finances, we must change our thinking.

We can have a *fixed* mindset we believe that our personal traits are fixed with little we can do to improve our lives. In contrast, we can have a *growth* mindset in that we believe that our personal traits are foundational toward our success. We can always improve our lives by defining what we want, learn about what we want and take actions to achieve what we want. Most people who have achieved any level of Financial Freedom have adopted the growth mindset.

In the book Secrets of the Millionaire Mind: Mastering the Inner Game of Wealth, T. Harv Eker offers 15 ways the rich think differently than the poor.

1. Rich people think big. Poor people think small.
2. Rich people believe "I create my life." Poor people believe "Life happens to me."
3. Rich people are committed to being rich. Poor people want to be rich.
4. Rich people play the money game to win. Poor people play the money game to not lose.
5. Rich people focus on opportunities. Poor people focus on obstacles.

6. Rich people admire other rich and successful people. Poor people resent rich and successful people.
7. Rich people associate with positive, successful people. Poor people associate with negative or unsuccessful people.
8. Rich people are willing to promote themselves and their value. Poor people think negatively about selling and promotion.
9. Rich people are bigger than their problems. Poor people are smaller than their problems.
10. Rich people choose to get paid based on results. Poor people choose to get paid based on time.
11. Rich people focus on their net worth.
12. Poor people focus on their working income.
13. Rich people manage their money well. Poor people mismanage their money.
14. Rich people have their money work hard for them. Poor people work hard for their money.
15. Rich people act in spite of fear. Poor people let fear stop them.
16. Rich people constantly learn and grow. Poor people think they already know."

As you can see from the statements above, the difference between the rich and the poor is not merely their Intelligence Quotient (IQ), its mindset. It's an attitude. It's what you think, learn and do with your time and money. Your mindset and your actions will determine your financial status.

7 Biggest Obstacles Preventing Financial Freedom

Learning how to overcome the obstacles preventing Financial Freedom was one of the lessons I learned from the Robert Kiyosaki Rich Dad's coaching program. My coach taught me six obstacles preventing Financial Freedom. (And I'm going to give you one more as a bonus!) Whether you know it or not, these obstacles impede your Financial Freedom. The quicker you master them, the quicker you can **Achieve Your Financial Goals**. In pursuing your financial freedom, here are 7 obstacles to overcome:

1. Disappointment
2. Fear
3. Bad habits
4. Laziness or lack of motivation
5. Criticism
6. Arrogance
7. Lack of financial education

As you take action to overcome these obstacles, you'll achieve your financial goals and transform your life!

How to Nurture Your Best Self to Transform Your Finances and Your Life

In Financial Freedom, mindset plays a major role. Mindset is a particular way of thinking, a belief, an attitude. Our thinking affects our financial decisions and results.

At times our mindset can be the biggest obstacle to Financial Freedom. When we have limited belief about money and wealth, we *repel* wealth from us. However, when we change our limited belief on wealth, we *attract* money.

One of the best ways to change your money mindset is to nurture your best self. The side of you that believes there is no limit in money. There's more than enough wealth for all. Here are 8 tips to nurture your best self to transform your life and your finances:

1. Define your vision and open your eyes to see all the opportunities around you that others do not see.
2. Develop a strategic plan to achieve your personal and professional goals. Get a life coach to help you as needed.
3. Develop a team to help you.
4. Develop courage by taking action toward your goals even when you feel afraid. Surround yourself with loving people.
5. Develop an attitude of gratitude. Be thankful for what you already have while pursuing new goals.
6. Take time off to pray, meditate and renew your thinking to be more creative.

7. Develop self-confidence to filter out criticism and negativity.
8. Develop self-control by delaying some gratifications.

As you master these tips, you'll nurture your best self to pursue Financial Freedom and transform your life!

7 Essential Money Skills

"Financial peace isn't the acquisition of stuff. It's learning to live on less than you make, so you can give money back and have money to invest. You can't win until you do this."
Dave Ramsey

There are 7 essential money skills that self-made millionaires practice to accumulate wealth. Since money creation is a skill, learn how to master these skills to achieve your Financial Freedom goals.

1. Value your money. It's an important tool to help you get what you need and want.
2. Make money with residual income from investment, by building businesses or getting a job.
3. Control every penny you have. If you are not controlling your money, it will soon control you.
4. Save. If you don't save your money when you don't need it, you won't have it when you need it. One of the best ways to save money is to automate it.
5. Invest to multiply your money. I recommend that you start with YOU! You are your best asset. Invest in your personal growth and development by getting a life coach. Real estate and businesses are great places to invest your money as well.
6. Protect your money by planning ahead.
7. Share your money with those in need by giving to your favorite charitable organizations.

Tips To Become a Millionaire

There's no secret formula to becoming financially free. It's your day-to-day financial decisions that determine whether you will become a millionaire or not. When most people start making more money than they need to meet their expenses, they often decide to buy more luxurious cars or move up to a larger or nicer home. If they took the extra money and invested it instead, they could become wealthy.

You can choose to become wealthy by adopting a millionaire mindset and take action toward your financial goals. You don't have to do it alone. Success is a team sport. Develop a team with professionals such as a life coach, financial planner, accountant or attorney to help you achieve your financial goals.

While there is no magic formula to becoming a millionaire, people who become one subscribe to the following tried-and-true method:

- Have a written financial plan that includes your goals, your net worth, your debt-to-income ratio, your savings and investing plans and your monthly budget.
- Manage your time and money wisely by following you're a plan
- Educate yourself about investing and developing businesses.
- Live within your means. Delay gratification for a bigger financial reward later.

- Avoid using credit cards unless you can afford your purchases, and will pay the balance off immediately.
- If you have credit card debt, concentrate on paying it off as quickly as possible. The interest you're paying could be going to your saving and investment accounts.
- Invest in targeted stock indexes and mutual funds, and have money deducted from your bank account automatically every month to invest in these funds.
- Own a profitable business.
- Enjoy everyday life with the most important people in your life.

In you want to obtain and maintain your Financial Freedom, commit to ongoing financial literacy and personal and professional development. As you can see, this proven method of becoming a millionaire is not rocket science. YOU can make into a reality.

What's Your Financial Status Now?

"Before you can improve your financial status, you must first know where you are now."
James Justin

Financial Freedom is a numbers game. The more you understand your numbers, the quicker you can improve them. There are a few important aspects of your financial statement that you simply cannot ignore. Neglecting these figures could be costly; but proactively working on them could lower your stress level; save you thousands of dollars and minimize future financial fiascos.

To improve your Financial Status, you must know the following 7 figures:

1. Your current monthly income
2. Your current monthly expenses. (The expenses must be managed to not exceed your income.)
3. Your annual assets
4. Your annual liabilities
5. Your debt level. (According to the U.S. National Debt Clock, the average American carries over $56,000 of debt. Do you know how much debt you currently have?)
6. Your credit score. (It may not seem that powerful, but your score could actually cost or save you thousands of dollars on your loans, as it is used to determine the interest rates attached to your loans and credit cards.)
7. Your Savings. (A 2014 Gallup poll of over 1,000 adults found that 59% of American adults are

worried about not having enough money for retirement, and 53% are worried about not being able to pay medical costs in the event of a serious illness or accident.)

Whether you love numbers or not, one thing is certain: knowledge of the seven numbers listed above can't be avoided if you want to be financially free.

If you are like me, you will realize the value of obtaining the services of a professional accountant to help you understand your financial statement. I can help you do that!

The more you understand these figures, the more prepared you'll be to make smart financial decisions.

What's Your Financial Goal?

*"People with goals succeed because
they know where they're going."*
Earl Nightingale

Once you understand your financial statement, the next step is to set smart goals to achieve your Financial Freedom. Along with goal setting, you must take actions to turn your goals into reality.

Success is a team sport. That's why I recommend getting a team to help you achieve your financial goals. In developing your team, I suggest getting professionals such as a success coach, financial planner, accountant and attorney to help you achieve your goals.

Before initiating any financial quest, consult your team and develop a plan to include your goal for security, comfort and beyond. Here are some goals to consider for your wealth building plan:

1. For your security plan, you can set a goal to make $5,000 per month (net) and follow the 30/70 rule discussed in this manual to manage your income effectively.
2. For your comfort plan, you can set a goal to make $10,000 per month.
3. For your rich plan, you can set a goal to make $100,000 per month.

As always, you have the power to choose which plan is best for you. Whatsoever plan you choose, pursue it with professional advisors and surround yourself with

63

loving people. Having a team will reduce stress, and save you time and money.

References

1. **Mindset: How To Transform Your Life From Ordinary To Extraordinary by James Justin**

   "All transforms begin in the mind. Therefore, if you change your mindset... You'll change your life!" Question... Is it possible for ordinary people to transform their lives to extraordinary? The answer is YES! Not only is it possible, but it's being done every day. This book is designed to show you how!

2. **How Successful People Think: Change Your Thinking, Change Your Life, book by John C. Maxwell**

   Gather successful people from all walks of life-what would they have in common? The way they think! Now you can think as they do and revolutionize your work and life!

   A Wall Street Journal bestseller, HOW SUCCESSFUL PEOPLE THINK is the perfect, compact read for today's fast-paced world. America's leadership expert John C. Maxwell will teach you how to be more creative and when to question popular thinking. You'll learn how to capture the big picture while focusing your thinking. You'll find out how to tap into your creative potential, develop shared ideas, and derive lessons from the past to better understand the future. With these eleven keys to more effective thinking, you'll clearly see the path to personal success.

3.Total Money Makeover, book by Dave Ramsey

Anyone who's listened to Dave Ramsey's radio show knows that he's all about common sense: avoid buying on credit, pay cash for everything possible, get yourself out of debt and build an emergency fund. Rather than airy-fairy promises and feel-good anecdotes, he offers sound, basic advice for the everyman and everywoman.

Best quote: *"What I have done is packaged the time-honored information into a process that is doable and has inspired millions to act on it."*

4.Financial Freedom: A Step-by-Step Practical Guide for Walking in God's Blessings, book by Terry Dean

Finally Learn the Shocking Truth about God's Plan for Your Financial Freedom. God's will for you is Financial Freedom. Yet a large percentage of Christians are barely making it from one week to the next. Why does it seem so hard to get ahead in life and why are so many believers living under a mountain of debt?

Find out about one young couple's journey from poverty and failure to prosperity and success. Learn why they were continually giving offerings, but only found themselves deeper in debt. They lived in a run-down rental house and had to search furniture just to find change to go out to eat at McDonald's.

Read about the one prayer that changed their lives forever. Soon their debts were paid off. They moved into a home with 18.5 acres which they paid off in less than a year. They gave more in offerings in one year's time than they used to earn combined in 3 years before.

Find out what they prayed and how this prayer could change your life forever. You've been taught God wants to prosper you, but you've never been given a step-by-step roadmap of how to get there. You've been told what God's will is, but you've never been taught HOW to accomplish it. In this step-by-step practical study, Terry Dean teaches you how to receive and walk in the blessings God has provided for you.

5. MONEY Master the Game: 7 Simple Steps to Financial Freedom, book by Tony Robbins

"If there were a Pulitzer Prize for investment books, this one would win, hands down" (Forbes.com). Based on extensive research and interviews with some of the most legendary investors at work today (John Bogle, Warren Buffett, Paul Tudor Jones, Ray Dalio, Carl Icahn, and many others), Tony Robbins has created a 7-step blueprint for securing financial freedom. With advice about taking control of your financial decisions, to setting up a savings and investing plan, to destroying myths about what it takes to save and invest, to setting up a "lifetime income plan," the book brims with advice and practices for making the financial game not only winnable—but providing financial freedom for the rest of your life. "Put MONEY on your short list of new books to read…It's that good" (Marketwatch.com).

6. Multiple Streams of Income: How to Generate a Lifetime of Unlimited Wealth, book by Robert Allen

In Multiple Streams of Income, bestselling author Robert Allen presents ten revolutionary new methods for generating over $100,000 a year—on a part-time basis, working from your home, using little or none of your own money. For this book, Allen researched hundreds of income-producing opportunities and narrowed them down to ten surefire moneymakers anyone can profit from. This revised edition includes a new chapter on a cutting-edge investing technique.

7. The Automatic Millionaire: A Powerful One-Step Plan to Live and Finish Rich, book by David Bach

What's the secret to becoming a millionaire?

For years, people have asked David Bach, the national bestselling author of Smart Women Finish Rich, Smart Couples Finish Rich, and The Finish Rich Workbook, what's the real secret to getting rich? What's the one thing I need to do?

Now, in The Automatic Millionaire, David Bach is sharing that secret.

The Automatic Millionaire starts with the powerful story of an average American couple--he's a low-level manager, she's a beautician--whose joint income never exceeds $55,000 a year, yet who somehow manage to own two homes debt-free, put two kids through college, and retire at 55 with more than $1 million in savings. Through their story, you'll learn the surprising fact that you cannot get rich with a budget! You have to have a plan to pay yourself first that is totally automatic, a plan that will automatically secure your future and pay for your present.

What makes The Automatic Millionaires unique?

- You don't need a budget
- You don't need willpower
- You don't need to make a lot of money
- You don't need to be that interested in money
- You can set up the plan in an hour

David Bach gives you a totally realistic system, based on timeless principles, with everything you need to know, including phone numbers and websites, so you can put the secret to becoming an Automatic Millionaire in place from the comfort of your own home. This one little book has the power to secure your financial future. Do it once--the rest is automatic!

8. Your Money or Your Life: 9 Steps to Transforming Your Relationship with Money and Achieving Financial Independence, book by Vicki Robin, Joe Dominguez and Monique Tilford

More than three-quarters of a million people everywhere, from all walks of life, have found the keys to gaining control of their money—and their lives—in this comprehensive and revolutionary book on money management.

9.The 4-Hour Workweek, book by Tim Ferriss

Flexible work hours are one of the chief points that drive individuals to begin their own businesses. This book explores the opportunities that you can get when you decide to take the plunge. And the way the author relates the points in a fun and motivational manner makes it all the more interesting.

10. Rich Dad, Poor Dad, book by Robert T. Kiyosaki and Sharon L. Lechter

An eighth-grade dropout who spends less than he earns is smarter than a college professor who can't make ends meet. According to Robert Kiyosaki, while working for a steady paycheck can get you started, your best investment of your time and money is to buy property or a business. Or better yet, do what Kiyosaki himself did and write a bestselling book.

Best quote: *"The key to Financial Freedom and great wealth is a person's ability or skill to convert earned income into passive income and/or portfolio income."*

11. Rich Dad's Guide to Investing: What the Rich Invest In, That the Poor and Middle Class Do Not! Book by Robert T. Kiyosaki

"Investing means different things to different people. In fact, there are different investments for the rich, poor, and middle class. Rich Dad's Guide to Investing is a long-term guide for anyone who wants to become a rich investor and invest in what the rich invest in. As the title states, it is a 'guide' and offers no guarantees…only guidance."
—Robert Kiyosaki

Rich Dad's Guide to Investing will reveal…

• Rich Dad's basic rules of investing
• How to reduce your investment risk
• Rich Dad's 10 Investor Controls
• How to convert your ordinary income into passive and portfolio income
• How you can be the ultimate investor
• How to turn your ideas into multimillion-dollar businesses
• How and why many people today will go bankrupt

12. Secrets of the Millionaire Mind, book by T. Harv Eker

If you're poor, it's because you think like a poor person, and if you're rich, it's because you think rich, according to author (and multi-millionaire) T. Harv Eker. To make matters worse, poor people essentially program their children to be poor, by providing them with a worldview that makes wealth accumulation impossible. Not to worry, though. If you start thinking like a mogul, you can be one, too.

Best quote: *"The vast majority of people simply do not have the internal capacity to create and hold on to large amounts of money and the increased challenges that go with more money and success."*

13. Think and Grow Rich, book by Napoleon Hill

Way back in the 1930s, the author interviewed a series of millionaires and philanthropists, starting with the steel magnate Andrew Carnegie. The result was a perennially best-selling work of self-development that encourages the notion that "greed is good," as long as you're willing to share your wealth.

Best quote: *"If you truly desire money so keenly that your desire is an obsession, you will have no difficulty in convincing yourself that you will acquire it. The object is to want money, and to be so determined to have it that you convince yourself that you will have it."*

14. The Science of Getting Rich, book by Wallace Wattle

Even though it contains nothing that even vaguely resembles "science," this 1910 book provided the intellectual framework for thousands of personal wealth-building seminars. Author Wallace Wattle believed that your ability to accumulate wealth is directly dependent upon how you think about it. In other words, if you believe that money is the root of all evil, you'll never be wealthy.

15. The Millionaire Next Door, book by Thomas J. Stanley and William D. Danko

Through research into U.S. households with a net worth of $1 million or more, the authors identify most individuals as Under Accumulators of Wealth (UAW) who have a low net wealth compared to their income. They then provide advice (like take skimpy vacations) to help people achieve a higher net worth compared to their income.

Best quote: *"People whom we define as being wealthy get much more pleasure from owning substantial amounts of appreciable assets than from displaying a high-consumption lifestyle."*

16.Click Millionaires: Work Less, Live More with an Internet Business You Love, book by Scott Fox

The rules have changed. The American Dream is no longer the "corner office." It's a successful lifestyle business you can run from your home office, the beach, or wherever you desire. It's work you love that still allows you the freedom and income to live the life you truly want. Sound like a tall order? Well, thanks to the Internet, anyone can launch a business with little or no start-up capital or technical expertise. And in Click Millionaires, lifestyle entrepreneurship expert Scott Fox teaches weary corporate warriors and aspiring entrepreneurs how to trade the 9-5 job they hate for an online business they love.

The book explains how to combine outsourcing, software, and automated   online marketing to build recurring revenues, all while working less and making fewer of the lifestyle compromises that corporate "success" requires. Readers will learn how to: find a lucrative niche on the Internet that matches their interests and skills; choose an online business model: from blogs, noozles, and online communities to digital delivery, online services, affiliate marketing-even physical products; position themselves as experts; build their audience; design the lifestyle they want; and balance passion and profits to realize their personal definition of success.

17. 7 Steps to Develop Healthy Relationship With Anyone, book by James Justin

"The health of your relationships will determine your level of success in life and in Business."

Success is a team sport. If you want to achieve your goals, enlist the help of your team. Team building is all about building relationships with people.

I invite you to embark on the journey to pursue healthy relationships. The benefits are worthwhile. Life is already so complicated; simplify it by developing healthy relationships. I have enjoyed the benefits of being in healthy relationships for years, and I hope for nothing less than the same for you! Let's get started with Justin's 7 Steps to Healthy Relationships:

- Become Self-Aware
- Become Selective
- Become the Friend You Want to Attract
- Become an Effective Communicator
- Become Loving
- Become Trustworthy
- Become Committed

18. The E-Myth Revisited: Why Most Small Businesses Don't Work and What to Do About It, book by Michael E. Gerber

In this first new and totally revised edition of the 150,000-copy underground bestseller, The E-

Myth, Michael Gerber dispels the myths surrounding starting your own business and shows how commonplace assumptions can get in the way of running a business. He walks you through the steps in the life of a business from entrepreneurial infancy, through adolescent growing pains, to the mature entrepreneurial perspective, the guiding light of all businesses that succeed. He then shows how to apply the lessons of franchising to any business whether or not it is a franchise. Finally, Gerber draws the vital, often overlooked distinction between working on your business and working in your business. After you have read The E-Myth Revisited, you will truly be able to grow your business in a predictable and productive way.

19.Business: How to Quickly Make Real Money-Effective Methods to Make More Money: Easy and Proven Business Strategies for Beginners to Earn Even More Money in Your Spare Time, book by Alex Nkenchor Uwajeh.

There are so many different ways to make money these days that you're almost spoilt for choice. Take a look at the options in this book and work out which one work best for your situation. You might just choose one or a combination of two or more options to build your business. You might even choose some of these options to help supplement your cash flow while you're building up another part of your overall business plan. No matter what you decide, the key to your success is creating a business model that works for you.

20. The Ten-Day MBA (4th Ed.): A Step-by-Step Guide to Mastering the Skills Taught In America's Top Business Schools, book by Steven A. Silbiger

Revised and updated to answer the challenges of a rapidly changing business world, the 4th edition of The Ten-Day MBA includes the latest topics taught at America's top business schools, from corporate ethics and compliance to financial planning and real estate to leadership and negotiation. With more than 400,000 copies sold around the world, this internationally acclaimed guide distills the lessons of the most popular business school courses taught at Harvard, Stanford, the University of Pennsylvania, the University of Chicago, Northwestern, and the University of Virginia. Author Steven A. Silbiger delivers research straight from the notes of real MBA students attending these top programs today—giving you the tools you need to get ahead in business and in life.

21. Selling 101: What Every Successful Sales Professional Needs to Know, book by Zig Ziglar.

Here in a short, compact and concise format are the basics of how to persuade more people more effectively, more ethically, and more often. Ziglar draws from his fundamental selling experiences and shows that while the fundamentals of selling may remain constant, sales people must continue learning, living, and looking: learning from the past without living there; living in the present by seizing each vital moment of every single day; and looking to the future with hope, optimism, and education. His tips will not only keep your clients happy and add to your income, but will also teach you ideas and principles that will, most importantly, add to the quality of your life. Content drawn from Ziglar on Selling.

22. Marketing In Less Than 1000 Words eBook by Marketing In Less Than 1000 Words, Kindle eBook by Rob Burns

Now over 40,000 downloads worldwide! A book on marketing you can read in 15 minutes flat. Under 1000 words, we explain the major principles of successful marketing - the absolute most important things you must understand to market your business successfully and find more customers. Each chapter is less than 70 words long. This is a book so short that everybody can make the time to read it.

About The Author

A born leader, James Justin hasn't let any obstacles stand in his way. And he has the skills and passion to make sure your obstacles are broken and no longer stand in *your* way.

"It's my passion to inspire and to help you transform your life to greater success, joy and happiness! This passion led me to earn my master's degree in the field of counseling and dedicate my life to speaking, coaching and helping people like you for over 20 years!"

James Justin is an entrepreneur, pastor, speaker, author and life coach. He earned his Master of Social Work (MSW) degree from Boston College, and his Bachelor of Social Work (BSW) degree from Eastern Nazarene College in Quincy, Massachusetts. He completed his public speaking training with the National Speakers Association Central Florida in 2014.

James worked as a professional counselor for the State of Florida for seven years prior to pursuing his passion and his dream: to help and make an impact in the private sector.

In 2011, James and his wife, Dr. Lauretta Justin co-authored and published their first book "Express Yourself!" In 2013, James published his solo book project titled "7 Steps to Develop Healthy Relationships With Anyone!" Other books by James include 12 Tips to Achieve Financial Freedom; Mindset: How To Transform Your Life From Ordinary To Extraordinary and Positive Parenting: 12 Practical Tips to Prepare your Kids for Success. James' books are available on his website, Amazon and where ever books are sold.

James and Lauretta are the proud parents of three incredible boys: Nathan, Sean and Joshua. They spend the majority of their free time focusing on "the boys!"

James is committed to helping create transformational growth with each and every one of his clients. To contact James, visit CoachJamesJustin.com!

www.ingramcontent.com/pod-product-compliance
Lightning Source LLC
Chambersburg PA
CBHW060636210326
41520CB00010B/1633